DANGEROUS MARINE ANIMALS
of the Pacific Coast

by

Christina Parsons

D1244149

Illustrated by Ron and Shira Stark

1986

Helm Publishing
San Luis Obispo, California

Sea Challengers
Monterey, California

The first aid information presented here is to help you prevent or relieve suffering. While every reasonable effort has been made to provide you with accurate information, no one involved with this book is responsible for or assumes liability for any action taken by any person using information in this guide. Anyone relying upon the first aid presented in this book does so at his or her own risk.

Library of Congress Catalog No. 85-81586

Helm Publishing ISBN 0-936940-03-4   Sea Challengers ISBN 0-930118-11-1
Helm Publishing is a division of Padre Productions

Distributed by: Aquacraft, BookLink Distributors, Baker & Taylor and others.
For information write: BookLink Distributors, P.O. Box 1275, San Luis Obispo, CA 93406.

Dedication

To my family—

"Love alone is capable of uniting living beings in such a way as to complete and fulfill them, for it alone takes them and joins them by what is deepest in themselves."

—Pierre Teilhard de Chardin

Contents

Cover photo: Moray Eel © by Daniel W. Gotshall
Book design: Lachlan P. MacDonald
Cover design: Jeff Nemeroff
Phototypesetting: Karen L. Reinecke

Foreword

Those of us fortunate enough to live by the ocean are able to witness on a daily basis the splendor of nature's diversity. We come to understand that the ocean is a myriad of life forms, constantly seeking survival. In time, we appreciate the evolutionary process each organism has achieved simply to be alive and to live in the sea.

It's not surprising, therefore, that as seaside residents we appreciate the defense mechanisms our ocean neighbors have developed. In fact, the existence of poisonous species is seen in terms of fragility rather than aggression. Because of this basic understanding, we learn to avoid rather than to challenge the creatures of the deep.

As a practicing emergency physician in a resort community, I see the unfortunate consequences of people's unfamiliarity with our ocean friends. All too often a visiting family will have its vacation interrupted because of an incident with a poisonous marine organism. All the more frustrating to me is how avoidable the accident could have been.

When Chris Parsons told me about her book, I first felt a sense of relief. With such a book, I would have a means to educate my patients and friends on the dangerous marine life of the Pacific. Moreover, Chris asked me to review her sections on first aid to be sure the advice was medically sound. As Chris completed her work, it became apparent that here was a practical and informative handbook. The information is succinct yet educational. The more I read, the more enthusiasm I had for her book.

Chris Parsons is well qualified to write on the subject of marine life. As a former biologist for the State of California Department of Fish and Game and a staff member of the Monterey Bay Aquarium, she is well-versed in Pacific marine life. Moreover, she saw the need for a quick, easy-to-use guide that would help the layperson avoid contact with toxic organisms. To her credit, she has fulfilled this need admirably.

It is always fulfilling for a physician to be able to prescribe something which will help prevent illness. By reading and referring to this book, the reader may well avoid an accident. In case, however, the reader should have need of immediate first aid, the book can also serve as a reference guide. As Ms. Parsons points out, when in doubt always seek medical attention.

The ocean is a vast and wondrous thing, magnetic to us in its appeal of relaxation and recreation. But like all things of nature, the ocean demands our respect and knowledge. As visitors to its boundaries, we can show our respect by understanding its more-dangerous side. By knowing which species of the deep one should avoid, we can maintain harmony between ourselves as vacationers and marine life as residents.

Robert P. K. Keller, M.D.
Emergency Medicine Expert
Carmel, California

Preface

One Saturday, while I was working for the State of California Department of Fish and Game, a fisherman came up to me and asked about bat rays. I asked him what he wanted to know about them. He wasn't sure. I noticed he was having trouble standing, his speech was slightly slurred, and he couldn't concentrate on our conversation very long. I assumed he had had a few-too-many beers.

His friends, who had been getting their boat on the trailer, came over and asked if bat rays were dangerous. I explained that the spine has venom and so should be avoided. Then the first fisherman showed me a two-inch cut on the palm of his hand. He said he had handled bat rays before and had never had any trouble with them; this was the first one that had ever "nicked" him. I suggested they get the man to an emergency room. He seemed to be having a severe reaction to the bat ray venom.

The fisherman insisted he was fine and on shaky legs he walked away.

Over the years I have encountered many fishermen, divers, and swimmers handling or about to handle a potentially dangerous marine animal with no idea of the hurt it could cause. I felt there was a need for a simple guide that would inform people of the danger. I had found some excellent books on dangerous marine life (see reference section, especially Halstead and Russell); however, none were written for the layperson. So I offer this guide to dangerous marine life in the hopes that there will be fewer injuries by, and more enjoyment of, our beautiful and fascinating marine animals.

As every author knows, a book is never completed without the aid and support of friends and colleagues. I would like to thank those who helped me: the injured fishermen, divers, and swimmers, for inspiring me to write this book; John Duffy of the State of California Department of Fish and Game, Chuck Farwell of the Monterey Bay Aquarium, Dr. Robert P. K. Keller, Harold Parsons, and David W. Behrens, for reviewing the manuscript and making helpful suggestions; Ron and Shira Stark, for their artistic talents and friendship; Suzanne Hall, for word processing and typing; Judy Rand, for proofreading, humor, and friendship; and Dan Gotshall of Sea Challengers, and Lachlan MacDonald, of Padre Productions, for their interest and faith in this project.

Introduction

Much of the recreation on the west coast of the United States is saltwater oriented. There is surfing, swimming, boating, fishing, snorkeling, SCUBA diving, tidepooling, and much more. With an increasing coastal population comes an increased use of the saltwater environment. The best way to enjoy this great resource is to know and avoid its hazards.

The objective of this book is to inform you, the saltwater user, about the biological hazards found in the waters off the west coast of North America. Marine organisms are not bound by political boundaries; this book is. It deals with dangerous animals found in waters off the United States and northern Baja California. What is harmless here may not be harmless in other areas. Outside the U.S., check with local authorities about the hazardous marine life of that area.

Although the overall danger from marine life is minimal, specific hazards can have extreme consequences. In most cases injury can be completely avoided if you are careful. You wouldn't consider a toothpick dangerous, yet if you handled it carelessly, it could injure you. The same is true for many marine animals; they can inflict injuries if you are not careful. Barnacles can cut your feet only if you walk barefooted on them; a salmon can bite your fingers only if you put them near its mouth.

Other marine animals have effective defense systems. They weren't developed to ruin your day at the beach; they're to help these animals survive in their world. To protect itself, an animal may flee, but it may also defend itself with whatever is available to it. As you will see in this book, some animals merely bite; a few, however, have very elaborate and sophisticated defense systems. If you are aware of what can hurt you, you can follow precautions so you don't get hurt.

Humans are not defenseless, however, peaceful coexistence is preferable to confrontation. Here are some general guidelines for avoiding dangerous encounters with marine life:

1. An animal will defend itself if it feels threatened or trapped, so don't touch, threaten, provoke, or attack a marine animal unless you are willing to pay the consequences.
2. Animals are unpredictable. Entering the animal world is like visiting a foreign land—you never fully understand the behavior or "customs." Therefore, never assume or try to predict what an animal will do next. Always be watchful and cautious; however, there is no need to be paranoid.
3. Think before you act.
4. Handle unfamiliar marine animals with extreme care and caution.
5. Carry a First Aid Kit. (See p. 84).
6. Learn First Aid procedures from your local chapter of the American Red Cross.
7. Remember, you are the visitor. The ocean is their home.

If your encounter with marine life results in injury to you, this book has some first aid suggestions for you. First aid is exactly that—immediate aid for an ill or injured person. It is only the first step in the treatment process. It is *not* a substitute for medical care.

First aid means action. Start by staying calm and by reassuring the victim. Then, treat life-threatening injuries—when there is no breathing or there is severe bleeding. Give mouth-to-mouth resuscitation, or CPR if needed, until breathing resumes. Stop severe bleeding by applying direct

11

pressure to the wound, using whatever clean absorbent material is available. Pressure on arteries and the use of a tourniquet should be used only in extreme cases when direct pressure isn't working.

If the victim's life is not in immediate danger, first aid should include calming the victim and keeping him or her lying down to prevent shock. Ask the victim what happened, examine the wound if there is one, and note the symptoms. Use the Table of Contents or the Index of this book to look up the animal that caused the injury or the major symptoms associated with marine life injuries. (The Table of Contents and the Index will direct you to the animals that inflict those kinds of symptoms or injuries.) Then you can follow the first aid procedures described. If you cannot determine what caused the injury, treat the more severe symptoms while making every effort to avoid further injury. If you are unsure or if the injury is severe, always seek medical attention.

This book is by no means the final or all-encompassing word on dangerous marine life in United States waters. It is intended to be a help in acquainting you—the fisherman, diver, boater, tidepooler, or bather—with some marine hazards and to advise you on how to handle them. For a more thorough treatment of this subject refer to the list of references at the end of this book.

The ocean is a beautiful and wonder-filled place enjoyed by millions of people each year. Be aware of the animals that make this their home, so your visits to the ocean can always be experiences to treasure.

I

INVERTEBRATES: INTRODUCTION

About 95% of all animals are invertebrates, that is, animals without backbones. Marine invertebrates familiar to most people are those served in restaurants: shimp, lobster, crab, clams, oysters, abalone, and squid.

Some people are allergic to shellfish (invertebrates with a shell like most of those listed above). When they eat these marine invertebrates, their body reacts to the shellfish protein. The reaction varies with each individual. Some people have mild reactions; some have very serious ones. Extreme sensitivity to the protein is called anaphylaxis. Allergy symptoms usually develop within a few hours of eating the shellfish. They may include weakness, flushness, itching or burning skin, vomiting, and difficult breathing. A person can go into shock (anaphylactic shock) and possibly die. Anyone with severe reactions should get medical attention. If you develop any of these symptoms, beware. You may be allergic to these foods and should stop eating them. If symptoms become severe, seek medical attention. For more information about anaphylaxis, talk to your physician.

The following pages describe invertebrates that are dangerous to everyone. These include invertebrates that are poisonous to eat, that have spines or sting, bite, and cut.

Invertebrates Poisonous to Eat
FILTER FEEDERS (CLAMS AND MUSSELS) AND DINOFLAGELLATES

DESCRIPTION: Dinoflagellates are microscopic organisms (neither plant nor animal) that are found in oceans throughout the world. They are most abundant during the warmer months of the year. Humans are usually not aware of their presence until large "blooms" occur. These blooms are known as red tide because they often color the water from yellow-brown to red. Many dinoflagellates are also bioluminescent and at night are seen as blue-green sparkles of light. Occasionally during a red tide there is a massive fish and invertebrate die-off in the immediate area. This may be due to a reduction of oxygen in the water.

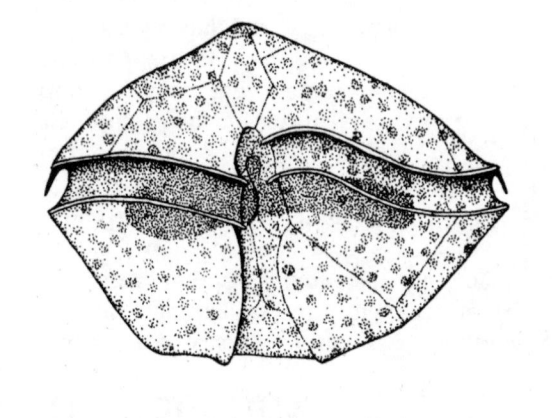

HAZARD: One species of dinoflagellate, known as *Gonyaulax catenella*, is filtered from the water and eaten by mussels, clams, and other filter feeders. The filter feeder stores and concentrates a toxin found in the dinoflagellate. This makes the filter feeder toxic to humans. This is one of the most deadly biological toxins and is commonly called paralytic shellfish poisoning.

PREVENTION: During the warm months of the year, usually May through October, do not eat filter-feeding animals, especially mussels or clams taken along this coast. Watch for posted quarantine notices. The presence or absence of a red tide will not help you predict danger, so check with your local Health Department or the State Department of Fish and Game before gathering clams or mussels. Cooking does not affect the toxin.

SYMPTOMS: Symptoms of paralytic shellfish poisoning usually develop within a few minutes of eating the toxic animal. The first signs are usually a tingling or numbness of the mouth and lips. This spreads to the face, fingers, and toes. A severe poisoning produces loss of muscle coordination, loss of speech, and breathing difficulties. Death occurs in 1 percent to 10 percent of the cases and is usually caused by the inability to breathe.

FIRST AID: Get immediate medical attention. If the victim stops breathing, give mouth-to-mouth resuscitation.

Invertebrates That Spine or Sting

SPONGES

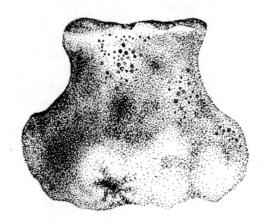

DESCRIPTION: Sponges are very primitive and simple animals that live attached to or encrusted on rocky or other hard surfaces. These animals are somewhat difficult to identify but basically all sponges have one or more small openings (oscules) on the body.

On this coast there are two species that can cause you harm. *Geodia mesotriaena* is white to gray. When young it tends to be spherical but becomes flattened and irregular up to 6 inches (15 cm) thick and 11 inches (28 cm) across. The surface appears "furry" but is hard and crusty. *Geodia* prefers crevices and caves along the shore to 1200 feet (370 m) deep.

Stelleta clarella is a feltlike uniformly white sponge often with a grayish surface. It grows to 3 inches (7.6 cm) thick and 18 inches (46 cm) across. This sponge lives along the shoreline from intertidal depths to depths of 80 feet (24 m).

HAZARD: Sponges have a supporting "skeleton" made of spicules or spines. These spicules are made of different substances. The two sponges described here have spicules made of silica or glass. The "glass" spicules when handled are like splinters that penetrate the skin and cause irritation.

PREVENTION: Do not handle sponges unless you are wearing gloves.

SYMPTOMS: Contact with these sponges produces pain and itchy, irritated skin.

FIRST AID: Using tweezers or adhesive tape, carefully remove the spicules. Wash the affected area and rinse with isopropyl alcohol. Topical cortisone may help relieve the pain. If infection occurs, get medical attention.

DESCRIPTION: A typical jellyfish has a bell shape and trailing tentacles. There are several dangerous species in our waters.

The lion's mane jellyfish (*Cyanea capillata*), one of the largest jellyfish, has a milky yellowish-brown bell [to 6 feet (2 m) diameter] with similarly-colored tentacles to over 100 feet (30 m).

The purple jellyfish (*Pelagia panopyra*) has a white body averaging one foot (30 cm) in diameter, with dark purple stripes. Tentacles may reach 20 feet (6 m).

The brown jellyfish (*Chrysaora melanaster*) has a yellow-brown bell to a foot (30 cm) in diameter, yellowish arms and brown tentacles to 6-8 feet (2-2.5 m) in length.

The common jellyfish *(Aurelia aurita)* is nearly colorless, with a bell to one foot (30 cm) diameter, bearing horseshoe-shaped markings around the center. It lacks long tentacles.

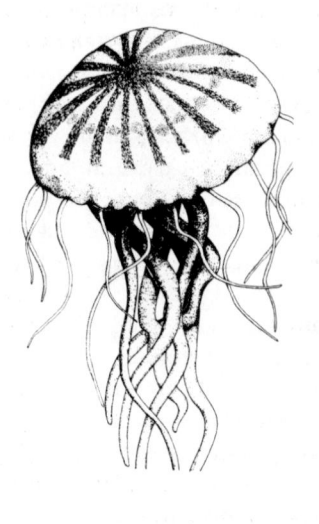

18

Jellyfish are normally found drifting in coastal waters, but, because they are weak swimmers, they can become trapped in currents and waves and washed onto the shore.

HAZARD: Jellyfish have stinging cells called nematocysts. These are located mostly on the tentacles, but are also on the bell. A nematocyst is a microscopic capsule that contains a coiled thread. There are many kinds of nematocysts: some have sticky threads; other have spines and venom for catching prey. When stimulated by direct contact or body chemicals, the nematocysts explode. You feel pain when the threads attach and inject venom. Skin contact with any part of the jellyfish can result in injury. This usually happens when a swimmer comes in contact with the tentacles or when someone steps upon or handles a jellyfish that has washed ashore.

PREVENTION: Do not let your skin come in contact with any part of a jellyfish. Beware of handling fishing lines or anchor ropes when you see jellyfish in the water.

SYMPTOMS: Contact with jellyfish nematocysts produces pain and skin irritations, such as itching, redness, swelling, and blisters.

FIRST AID: Do NOT rub or rinse with fresh water. This may cause more nematocysts to fire. Immediately apply isopropyl alcohol or vinegar to the injured area to deactivate stinging cells. With towel or tweezers, pull off any pieces of jellyfish that may be on the skin. Sprinkle meat tenderizer containing papain over the wound to relieve pain. Topical cortisone may also be helpful in relieving some of the discomfort. Recovery depends on the severity of the symptoms. It may take only a few hours or a few days. If severe symptoms develop or persist, get medical attention.

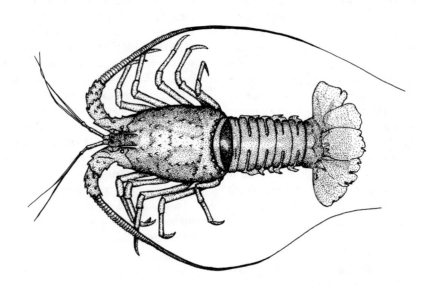

SPINY LOBSTER *Panulirus interruptus*

DESCRIPTION: The spiny lobster is identical to other lobsters, except that it lacks giant claws. It is colored various shades of red. The spiny lobster lives in rocky areas in caves and under ledges from along the shore to 200 feet deep (60 m). These lobsters grow to a maximum of 3 feet (1 m) in length.

HAZARD: Although the spiny lobster does not have claws, it can inflict injury to those attempting to capture or handle one. As the name implies, this lobster is covered with spines. These spines are located along the antennae, above the eyes, on the back, and along the sides of the tail. Grabbing a spiny lobster or allowing the tail to curl around your fingers may cause puncture wounds or cuts. Sport divers or anglers with ring nets are most likely to encounter one and should be aware of the hazards.

PREVENTION: Wear gloves when handling spiny lobsters and handle with care. Do not let the tail curl around your fingers.

SYMPTOMS: Carelessly handling a spiny lobster may result in puncture wounds and cuts.

FIRST AID: Clean wounds and apply a topical antibiotic. If cuts are severe, get medical attention for suturing.

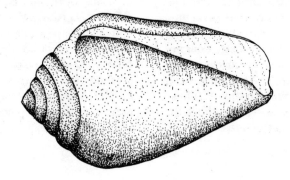

CALIFORNIA CONE SNAIL *Conus californicus*

DESCRIPTION: The California cone snail is a small (about 1 inch [2.5 cm]) snail with a dull brownish, cone-shaped shell. The opening in the shell is approximately 80% of the shell length. This cone snail is found in rocky and sandy areas along the shore to 150 feet (45 m) deep.

HAZARD: Cone snails, especially those that eat fish, possess venom and use their sharp, microscopic needlelike teeth to inject the venom into their prey. Whether the snail "stings" or "bites" is a matter of debate. The California cone snail has *not* been known to injure humans; however, all cone snails should be handled with care.

PREVENTION: Wear heavy gloves when handling cone snails. Do not place cone snails in pockets or other areas close to the body.

SYMPTOMS: A sting by a cone snail produces a single puncture wound. This is followed by immediate pain and swelling, then numbness. Severe symptoms from tropical species include weakness, paralysis, and in some cases, difficult breathing and death.

FIRST AID: Clean the wound. To relieve the pain soak the wound in the hottest water the victim can tolerate. Apply an antibiotic. If severe symptoms develop or persist, get medical attention.

SEA URCHIN *Strongylocentrotus* spp.

DESCRIPTION: Sea urchins possess a round test (shell) covered with spines, tube feet, and pedicellariae (pincers). Spine color, shape, and length vary. There are several species found off our coast. The most common are the red and purple sea urchins. The red sea urchin has long, slender, red to dark purple spines. This urchin grows to 8 inches (20 cm) in diameter. The red sea urchin is common in rocky reef areas from shore to 100 feet (30 m).

The purple urchin has short, bright blue to light purple spines. This urchin grows to a maximum of 4 inches (10 cm) in diameter. The purple urchin is found on rocky bottoms from the shore to 80 feet (24 m).

24

HAZARD: Sea urchin spines are used for protection, among other things. They can penetrate a wet suit or the sides of tennis shoes, causing puncture wounds. Sea urchin spines are very brittle and often break off in a wound. Local species are not venomous.

PREVENTION: Care should be taken in urchin areas. Look before stepping so you don't step on one. When diving, look before reaching to avoid impaling yourself on an urchin. Handle urchins with extreme care.

SYMPTOMS: Most people have no reactions to sea urchin spines, except for the initial pain when pierced. Spines within wounds should be removed; however, because of the brittleness of the spine, some pieces usually remain in the wound. These are generally absorbed within several days. In some cases there is a reaction to the porous spine. Symptoms include redness, swelling, some pain and bacterial infection around the wound.

FIRST AID: Wash the wound and remove any surface spines. If a reaction develops, get medical attention.

SEA PORCUPINE or HEART URCHIN *Lovenia cordiformis*

DESCRIPTION: The sea porcupine looks somewhat like a flattened sea urchin. It is oval shaped with beige-to-lavender-colored spines radiating from front to back. The sea porcupine is found half-buried in sandy areas in extreme low tide zones. It gets no longer than approximately 3 inches (7.5 cm).

HAZARD: The long spines of the sea porcupine are believed to contain a venom.

PREVENTION: Do not handle the sea porcupine with bare hands. Wear shoes when wading in sandy flats where this species lives, especially at low tide.

SYMPTOMS: The venom associated with the spines causes pain and redness.

FIRST AID: Soak the wounded area in the hottest water the victim can tolerate to stop the pain. If symptoms are severe, get medical attention.

Invertebrates That Bite

BLOODWORM *Glycera dibranchiata*

DESCRIPTION: Bloodworms are reddish, segmented earthwormlike animals. (The body fluids resemble blood, hence the name). These worms grow to about 8 inches (20 cm) in length. The head contains a retractable proboscis (snout) which can be extended to about 1/5 the body length. At the end of this snout are four jaws or fangs. Bloodworms are found in burrows in soft muddy areas along the coast. They are used by fishermen for bait.

HAZARD: Each of the fangs on the bloodworm's snout comes complete with a venom gland that opens into the base of the fang. Bloodworms do bite when disturbed or handled. This bite is venomous and painful. Bloodworms are most hazardous to fishermen collecting or using them for bait.

PREVENTION: Handle bloodworms with extreme care. Gloves should be worn.

SYMPTOMS: A bite from a bloodworm usually results in pain, swelling, and redness. Two to four cuts are usually present.

FIRST AID: Clean the wound. If there is a great deal of pain, soak the wound in the hottest water the victim can withstand for 30 to 90 minutes. Then apply an antibiotic. If infection or complications arise, get medical attention. Complete recovery usually occurs within a few days.

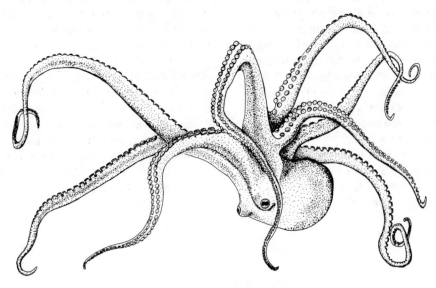

OCTOPUS *Octopus* spp.

DESCRIPTION: The octopus has a fleshy baglike body and eight arms with suction cups. In our coastal waters, below the tide zone, an octopus' armspread (from the tip of one arm to the tip of the opposite arm) can be as much as 10 feet (3 m); however, the armspread of most is about 2 to 3 feet (1 m). The suction cups on the arms are used for grasping, holding, and tasting prey. Small (1″ to 12″) octopus are common in rocky intertidal areas along the shore. Their color varies and can change rapidly, usually to blend with the surroundings.

HAZARD: Humans greatly exaggerate the danger posed by octopus. Although the octopus possesses a parrotlike beak and venom apparatus, it does not attack humans. Those found in our coastal waters will seldom bite, even when handled.

PREVENTION: Do not handle an octopus. If you must, wear gloves and be careful of the beak.

SYMPTOMS: An octopus bite will leave puncture wounds, usually two. There may be some pain, swelling, tingling, redness, and itching.

FIRST AID: Clean the wound and apply a topical antibiotic. If symptoms are severe, immerse the wounded area in the hottest water the victim can tolerate. Then get medical attention.

Invertebrates That Cut

BARNACLES *Balanus* spp. and others

DESCRIPTION: A barnacle is basically a shrimp in a shell on a rock. All you usually see of the barnacle are the plates which provide a protective wall around the animal. The shell is small (up to ½ inch [1.2 cm]) and of a whitish color. Barnacles usually occur in enormous numbers blanketing the rocks.

HAZARD: The shell of the barnacle is sharp and irregular. Injury usually occurs when you walk with naked feet across barnacle-covered rocks. SCUBA divers should be aware of barnacles when diving in surgy shallow areas.

PREVENTION: Wear shoes when walking through tidepools and/or across rocky areas along the shore.

SYMPTOMS: Barnacle shells can cause jagged cuts or tears, bleeding, and bruises.

FIRST AID: If the bleeding is severe, apply direct pressure to stop it. Wash the wounded area and apply a topical antibiotic. If the cuts are severe or become infected, get medical attention.

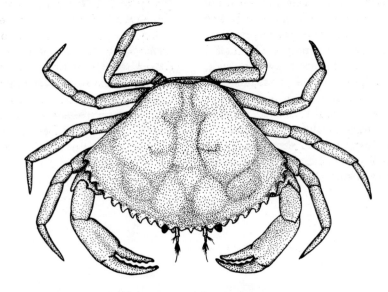

CRABS *Cancer* spp. and others

DESCRIPTION: There are many species of crab found off our coast. All have a hard shell and ten legs (two of which are pincer-like claws called chelae). Crabs are usually found on sand or mud bottoms as well as in protected areas, such as rocky ledges or dense plant growth.

HAZARD: Claws enable crabs to defend themselves against aggressors, including humans. Most crabs can be grasped safely by the middle of the back; however, some crabs are very limber and you may find yourself caught by a crab instead of catching one. Kelp crabs have spines which can cut or puncture, similar to those inflicted by barnacles.

PREVENTION: Handle crabs at your own risk. Gloves may protect skin from the claws of smaller individuals, but will do little to protect against the crushing abilities of large ones.

SYMPTOMS: A provoked crab can produce cuts, bleeding, bruises, and pain.

FIRST AID: Wash the wounded area. Use direct pressure on the wound to stop bleeding. If area is badly bruised use cold packs. Get medical attention for any serious wounds.

II

FISHES: *INTRODUCTION*

Fishes are simply a group of vertebrates (animals with backbones) which live in the water and have gills for breathing. A few species defend themselves with body parts or behaviors which can be dangerous to the unwary person.

There are three major groups of fishes. One group, the jawless fishes, is not represented in this book. The other two groups are: the cartilaginous fishes, which include sharks, skates, rays, and ratfishes; and the bony fishes, which include all the more typical fishes.

See fish anatomy (p. 40).

In general, cartilaginous fishes have no bones: their skeletons are made of cartilage, like the material forming the bridge of your nose. These fishes have several pairs of gill openings and the scales (of those that have scales) are toothlike and do not overlap.

Bony fishes have a calcified skeleton, as we commonly see in animal bone. They have a single pair of gill openings covered by a gill cover called the operculum. Most bony fishes have scales that overlap one another.

Any fish with teeth and spines can inflict harm if improperly handled. All fish, whether alive or dead, should be handled with care. Special attention should be given to avoiding the mouth and teeth, spines along the dorsal, pelvic, and anal fins, raised areas on the head, near the tail, and on the gill cover (operculum). Swordfish and sailfish in or out of the water should be treated with great respect and handled with extreme care. They possess a powerful spear that can pierce wood planking, boat hulls, and human body parts.

Some fishes are poisonous to eat. We are fortunate that very few fishes in our coastal waters possess such toxins. These toxins may be produced by bacteria, by toxic plants or animals that the fish has eaten (ciguatera poisoning), or by pollutants in the water. You can avoid some forms of poisoning by taking care where you fish. Before going fishing check with your local Health Department, especially during the summer months, for information on toxic fishes in your area. If, after eating fish, you develop flulike symptoms such as stomach cramps, nausea, vomiting, headache, dizziness, weakness, or muscle aches, seek medical attention.

Stay out of waters closed due to pollution. Fish only in clean, uncontaminated waters. Keep your catch in circulating sea water until you clean it, if possible. Otherwise, clean your fish very soon after catching, by removing the gills and internal organs (stomach, intestines, kidneys, etc.). Then refrigerate or ice your catch.

Other poisonings you need to concern yourself with are tetradon or pufferfish poisoning (see p. 47), scombroid poisoning (see p. 43), elasmobranch or shark poisoning (see p. 39), and cabezon egg poisoning (see p. 45).

The following pages describe commonly encountered fishes that are poisonous to eat, that have spines or can sting or bite.

Fishes Poisonous to Eat

ELASMOBRANCH (SHARK) POISONING

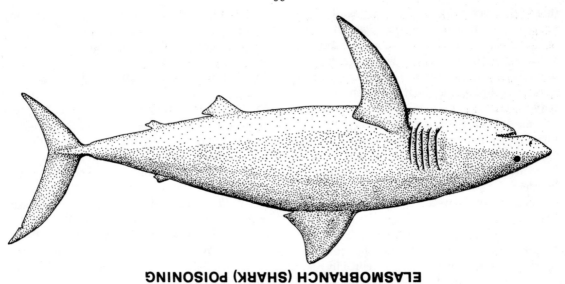

HAZARD: Some sharks are poisonous to eat. This is especially true of tropical species. The liver seems to be the most toxic part of the shark. Some scientists believe that eating the liver of sharks results in an overdose of vitamin A and this is what causes the poisoning.

PREVENTION: Do not eat the liver of sharks.

SYMPTOMS: Within about 30 minutes of eating shark liver you may have nausea, vomiting, diarrhea, stomach pain, headache, cold sweats, weakness, muscle cramps, and breathing difficulties. Severe symptoms include coma and death.

FIRST AID: None. Get immediate medical attention.

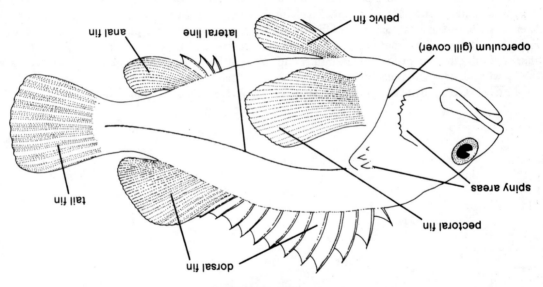

Typical Fish

FISHES WITH WORMS

Fish, like all animals, have parasites. Some are found externally and can be removed easily. These should not affect the quality of the meat. Some parasites are found in the gills, stomach, or intestines. These are normally discarded when the fish is cleaned and so have no effect.

The parasites of most concern to fishermen and divers are the small white "worm cysts" or "grubs" found within the meat. These "worms" are usually one stage or form of life in the complex life cycle of a parasite. The presence of these parasites usually does not affect the quality of the fish meat. To see if there are worms in the meat, hold thinly sliced pieces up to the light. The parasites will appear as shadows. If they offend you, you can remove them from the meat before cooking. Thorough cooking or smoking should, however, eliminate any danger from these parasites. Eating raw fish that contains parasites is not recommended. Freezing the fish at -40°F for 24-60 hours should make raw fish safe to eat. You can get more information on parasites in fish from *Common Parasites of California Marine Fish* by Moser, Love and Sakanari available from the State of California Department of Fish & Game.

TUNAS, SKIPJACKS AND BONITOS

HAZARD: A toxin can occur in members of the scombroid family, which includes tunas, albacore, skipjacks, and bonitos. If these animals are inadequately preserved after being caught, a toxic substance, probably caused by bacteria, will develop in the meat.

PREVENTION: Clean these fish immediately after catching, then put on ice or refrigerate. Do not eat these fish if the meat has a peppery taste.

SYMPTOMS: Eating toxic scombroids produces nausea, vomiting, diarrhea, stomach pains, dizziness, headaches, thirst, and burning of the throat. Breathing difficulty develops in severe cases. These symptoms usually develop within two hours after eating the meat and usually disappear within 8 to 12 hours.

FIRST AID: Get medical attention immediately.

CABEZON *Scorpaenichthys marmoratus*

DESCRIPTION: The cabezon is one of the largest members of the sculpin family. The body of the cabezon is without scales, so the skin is smooth and wrinkled. The color varies from reddish to greenish with mottling over the entire body. The head is broad and there is a fleshy flap (cirrus) in the middle of the snout and over each eye. The cabezon can grow to 39 inches (1 m) in length. Cabezon occur from the shore to about 250 feet (75 m) deep around reefs and kelp beds.

HAZARD: The eggs (roe) of the cabezon are poisonous.

PREVENTION: Do not eat the eggs of the cabezon. The meat is safe to eat.

SYMPTOMS: Eating cabezon roe produces nausea, vomiting, and diarrhea. Complete recovery usually occurs in a few days.

FIRST AID: Get medical attention.

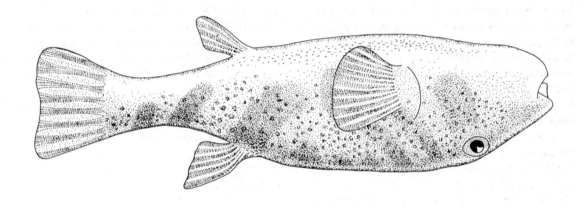

PUFFERS AND PORCUPINEFISH

DESCRIPTION: Puffers and porcupinefish are also known as balloonfish or swellfish because of their ability to inflate themselves into a balloon by swallowing water or air. This is done to protect themselves from their enemies. Puffers and porcupinefish are not more than a few feet in length. Some have smooth skin; others are covered with burrs or spines. Most commonly found in warmer waters, these fish are very rare along our coast.

HAZARD: Puffers and porcupinefish are probably the most toxic of all fishes, causing many deaths each year. The amount of toxin within the fish varies according to species, part of the body, time of the year, and where it was caught. The reproductive organs, liver, and intestines are the most toxic parts of the fish. Poisoning by these fish is called tetradon poisoning.

PREVENTION: Do not eat any part of a puffer or porcupinefish.

SYMPTOMS: Eating toxic parts of these fish produces a tingling of the lips, tongue, and throat. The victim may also feel dizziness, nausea and numbness. They may have uncoordinated movements and breathing difficulties. Severe symptoms include a drop in blood pressure, paralysis, and death. Death results within 6 to 24 hours after eating the fish, from an inability to breathe.

FIRST AID: There is no known "cure" for tetradon poisoning; however, the victim should still get medical attention immediately. If breathing stops, give the victim mouth-to-mouth resuscitation.

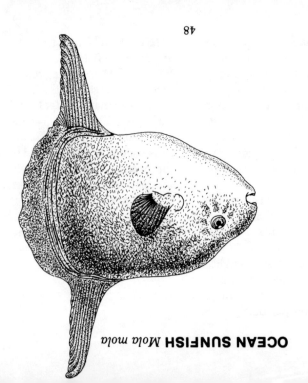

OCEAN SUNFISH *Mola mola*

DESCRIPTION: The ocean sunfish or mola is an open-ocean fish seen lying on the surface of the water. Molas are silvery, oval shaped, lack a tail fin, have a tiny mouth, and long dorsal and anal fins set well back on the body. These fish are found in temperate and tropical waters of the world. They can grow to 13 feet (4 m) in length.

HAZARD: Molas may contain the same toxin as puffers and porcupinefish.

PREVENTION: Do not eat any part of the mola.

SYMPTOMS: Eating toxic parts of these fish produces a tingling of the lips, tongue, and throat. The victim may also feel dizziness, nausea and numbness. They may have uncoordinated movements and breathing difficulties. Severe symptoms include a drop in blood pressure, paralysis, and death. Death results within 6 to 24 hours after eating the fish, from an inability to breathe.

FIRST AID: Get medical attention immediately. If breathing stops, give mouth-to-mouth resuscitation.

Fishes That Spine or Sting

ROUND STINGRAY *Urolophus halleri*

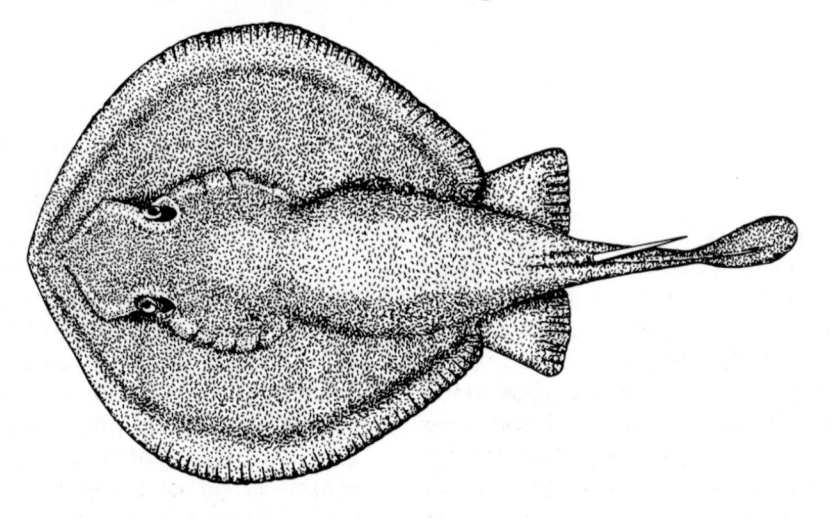

DESCRIPTION: There are several species of rays along this coast, but the stingray and the bat ray are the most common. Rays have flattened bodies, usually dark on the back and light on the underside. Some species of rays, including these, have a barbed, venomous spine on the tail. This spine is covered with an integumental sheath (a thin layer of skin). When this sheath is broken, the venom flows out. Round stingrays grow to about 22 inches (56 cm); bat rays to a 4-foot (1.2 m) wing span. These rays generally live on sandy or muddy bottoms along beaches, bays, and sloughs in a few inches of water to offshore depths of more than 100 feet (30 m).

HAZARD: These rays possess a venomous spine as a defense weapon. A stingray usually inflicts injury when a swimmer accidentally steps on it. When a stingray is stepped on, it bends its tail forward toward the intruder, usually wounding the foot or ankle. This breaks the sheath and the venom enters the wound. Stingrays and bat rays inflict venomous wounds when they are captured by fishermen and handled carelessly.

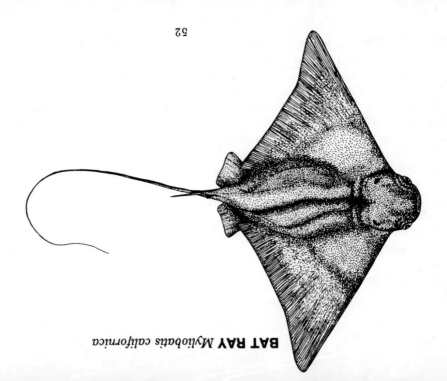

BAT RAY *Myliobatis californica*

PREVENTION: When wading in water along sandy or muddy beaches or bays, wear boots or shuffle your feet to scare off any stingrays. Be cautious when jumping up and down in the water —you don't want to land on a stingray. If you catch a stingray or bat ray, handle it with extreme care by avoiding the tail.

SYMPTOMS: Being spined by a stingray or bat ray produces immediate pain. Because the spine is barbed, there are usually cuts and bleeding. The pain may be accompanied by nausea, vomiting, muscle cramps or weakness.

FIRST AID: Wash the wound. Remove any remains of the integumental sheath, if present. Immerse the wound in the hottest water the victim can tolerate for 30 to 90 minutes. Medical attention is often necessary to suture the wound and give antibiotics.

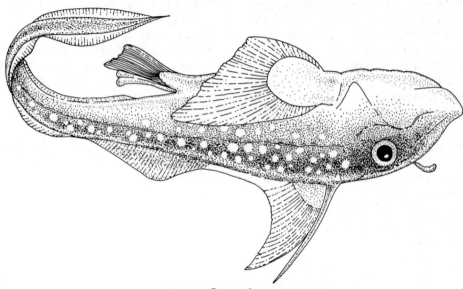

RATFISH *Hydrolagus colliei*

DESCRIPTION: The body of the ratfish is white to silver with numerous light spots. There are also dark silver-to-bronze metallic hues on the skin. The skin has no scales and the bones are mostly made of cartilage, which makes them weak and pliable. The tail is very thin, almost eel-like. The ratfish grows to a length of 3 feet (1 m) and is found from shallow waters to depths of 1200 feet (360 m). Divers and fishermen, except trawler fishermen, rarely see this fish.

HAZARD: The ratfish has a large, serrated, venomous spine at the origin of the dorsal fin. Males have a spiny club-shaped process on the forehead and sharp clasping organs adjacent to pelvic fins. It also has incisor-like teeth and has been known to bite.

PREVENTION: Handle the ratfish with care. Avoid the dorsal spine, forehead, teeth, and pelvic area.

SYMPTOMS: The spines of the ratfish produce puncture wounds that can be very painful. A bite or clasp from a ratfish can produce punctures and cuts.

FIRST AID: Wash the wound. Use direct pressure on the wound to stop any bleeding. If the wound is painful, place it in the hottest water the victim can tolerate. If infection develops or symptoms persist, get medical attention.

CALIFORNIA SCORPIONFISH *Scorpaena guttata*

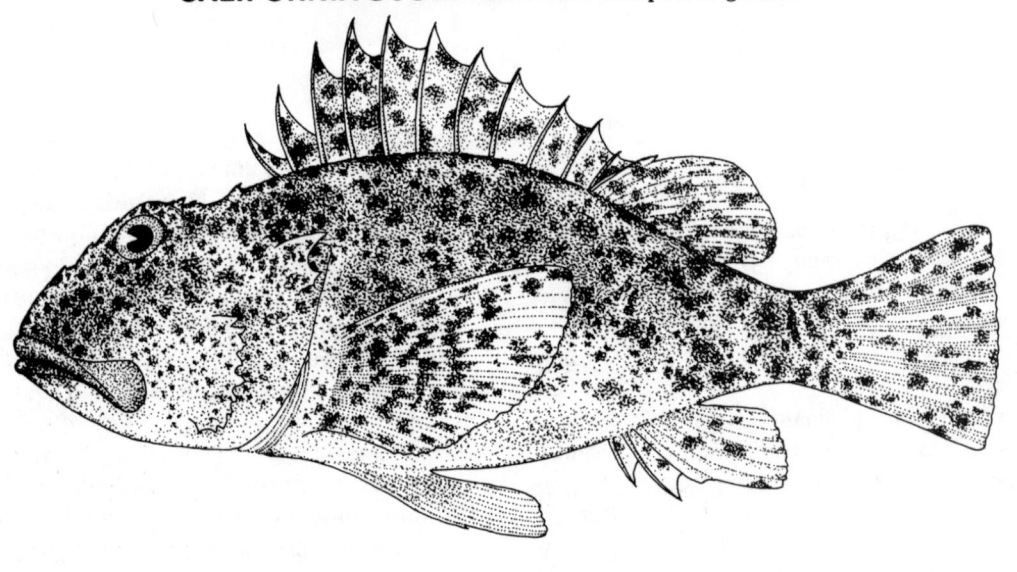

DESCRIPTION: The California scorpionfish has a large spiny head, brick-red to reddish-brown-colored body with dark spots and blotches, and twelve short, heavy dorsal spines. These fish occur from the shore to about 600 feet (180 m) in rocky areas. California scorpionfish grow to about 17 inches (40 cm) in length.

HAZARD: California scorpionfish have venomous spines in the dorsal, anal, and pelvic fins. Most stings occur when this fish is being removed from a hook, from a fishing bag, or when being cleaned.

PREVENTION: Handle a California scorpionfish, if you must, with extreme care; avoid the dorsal, anal, and pelvic fins.

SYMPTOMS: Being spined by a California scorpionfish results in almost immediate and extreme pain around the wound. This pain will quickly spread to surrounding areas. The area around the wound usually becomes red and puffy. Nausea, vomiting, weakness, headache and diarrhea may develop. If not treated, the pain will usually subside in 3 to 8 hours. Tenderness around the wounded area may persist for a few days.

FIRST AID: Clean the wound. Immerse the wounded area in the hottest water that the victim will tolerate until the pain stops. Use a topical antibiotic on the wound to prevent infection. If pain persists or if symptoms are severe, get medical attention.

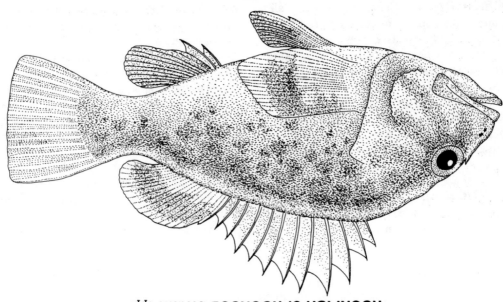

ROCKFISH or ROCKCOD *Sebastes* spp.

DESCRIPTION: There are approximately 60 species of rockfish found off this coast. They are the major part of the total fish catch here. Rockfish come in a variety of sizes and colors and from a variety of habitats making individual species sometimes difficult to identify. Rockfish usually have large eyes, broad heads, head spines, and 13 dorsal spines.

HAZARD: Rockfish, along with the California scorpionfish, belong to the scorpionfish family (see preceding fish). All of the species possess venomous spines. Although the rockfish venom is not as potent as that of the California scorpionfish, it does cause reactions in some people.

PREVENTION: Handle rockfish with great care avoiding the spines, particularly the dorsal spines.

SYMPTOMS: Being spined by a rockfish may produce pain, swelling, and redness.

FIRST AID: Clean the wound. If pain is severe, soak the wounded area in the hottest water the victim can tolerate until the pain stops. Use a topical antibiotic to prevent infection.

Fishes That Bite

SHARKS

BLUE SHARK *Prionace glauca*

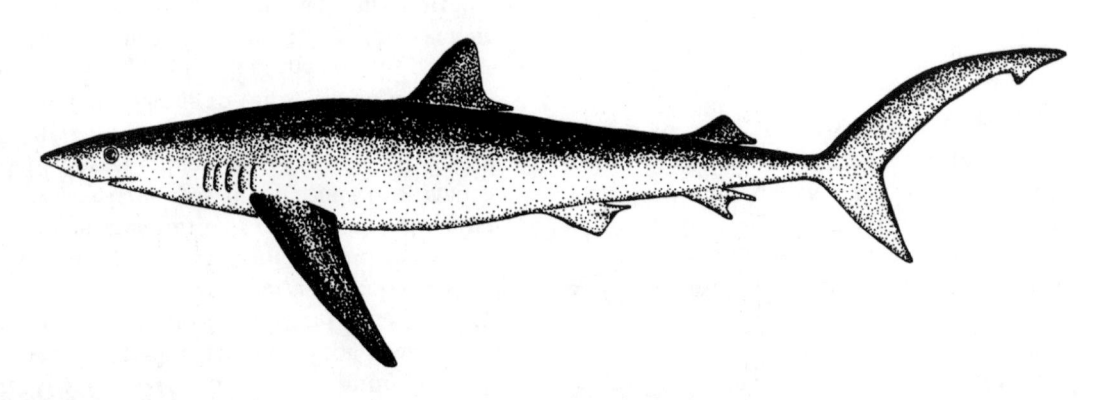

DESCRIPTION: Approximately thirty-five species of shark live off this coast. (This number does not include skates and rays.) Of the thirty-five, however, only eight have been known to attack people. They are: the tiger shark, blue shark, bull shark, dusky shark, pelagic white-tipped shark, bonito shark, great white shark, and hammerhead shark.

The sharks found off this coast are either pelagic (open ocean) or bottom dwellers. Pelagic sharks have streamlined, torpedo-shaped bodies and are usually dark on the back, getting progressively lighter toward the underside. Bottom-dwelling sharks have a more flattened shape than their pelagic relatives. This enables them to swim over and rest on the bottom more easily. Bottom-dwelling sharks are usually colored to blend with their surroundings.

Sharks are predators. Most have several rows of very sharp, triangular-shaped teeth. Teeth from the back rows continually rotate forward to replace teeth lost from the front row.

HAZARD: Shark attacks on humans, although much publicized, are rare. Because sharks are predators, they have very acute senses of smell and hearing, which includes a system for detecting vibrations in the water like those produced by a struggling or injured fish. The acuteness of the sharks' sight is much debated, but they probably see well within 50 feet of an object and may be attracted to movements especially those of light objects moving past dark backgrounds. Sharks, even small ones, bite, especially when they are harassed or injured.

BONITA SHARK *Isurus oxyrinchus*

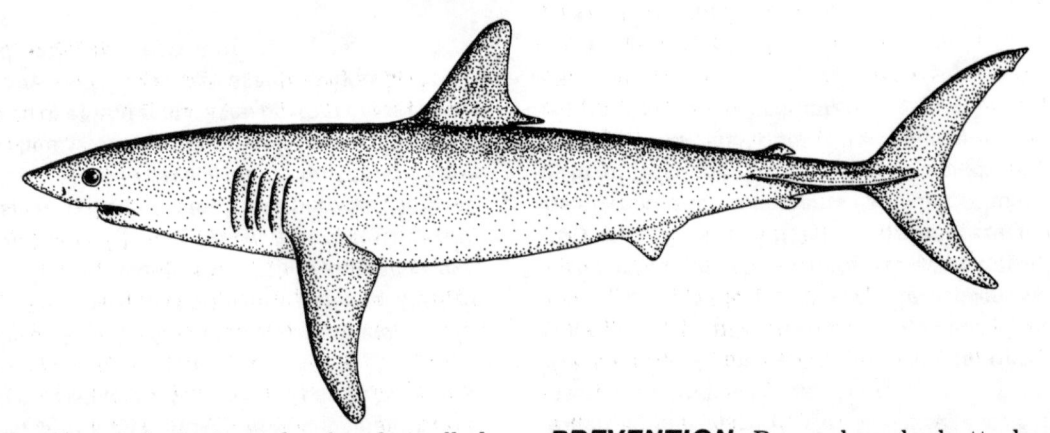

The skin of sharks is made of scales called dermal denticles, meaning "skin teeth." Brushing against the skin can cause serious cuts and scrapes.

PREVENTION: Remember, shark attacks on people are rare. Although no shark attack prevention is 100% effective, these tips will reduce your chances of attracting or aggravating sharks.

Don't swim in a known shark area, such as around seal or sea lion breeding grounds, unless you have to. Don't swim in areas where shark attacks have occurred recently. Splashing or swimming erratically may attract sharks so try to keep your movements quiet and rhythmical. If you see a pelagic shark while you are in the water, get out of the water as soon as possible by moving cautiously and methodically so you don't attract the shark. Don't swim with bleeding wounds. Don't carry bleeding or wounded fish closely attached to your body. Place speared fish in a boat or raft while you're diving. Don't poke, grab, or otherwise harass any species of shark. Many shark attacks occur because a person has attacked the shark first. Take a buddy with you when swimming or diving. That way help is available if you should need it.

SYMPTOMS: Shark skin may cause scrapes or cuts. A bite from a shark may result in puncture wounds and severe cuts. These can be painful and cause great blood loss. Shark attack victims often suffer from shock. Human death has resulted from shark attacks in about 35% of the cases.

FIRST AID: Remain calm and assure the victim. Get the victim out of the water as quickly as possible. Stop any bleeding by applying direct pressure to the wound with any clean absorbent material. Use your hand if nothing else is available. Pressure on arteries or a tourniquet should be used only when the bleeding is too severe to be stopped with direct pressure. Treat the victim for shock by keeping him or her quiet and lying down and by covering him or her just enough to prevent heat loss. If you use a tourniquet, do not cover it. Rush the victim to medical help.

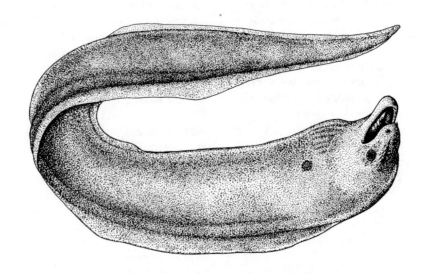

CALIFORNIA MORAY EEL *Gymnothorax mordax*

DESCRIPTION: Moray eels (or morays, as they are commonly called) are eel-shaped fish commonly found in rocky areas from shallow water to about 130 feet (40 m). They spend days in rocky holes and crevices and search for food at night. Underwater they usually look as if they are ready to attack; the head is poking out of the hiding place and the mouth is wide open showing the sharp teeth. This behavior is not to threaten you, but enables the moray to breathe. Moray eels do not have large open gills like most fishes. They open and close their mouths to pump water over the gills. Morays grow to about 5 feet (1.5 m) in length.

HAZARD: The danger to divers from moray eels is greatly exaggerated. California morays do not attack humans unless provoked. Moray eels do bite. Many bites occur when divers, in search of abalone or lobsters, place a hand into a moray's cave. The moray often bites, either to protect its home or to taste the morsel that has just entered its home.

PREVENTION: Look carefully before reaching into holes or crevices. Do not challenge, provoke, or spear a moray.

SYMPTOMS: Bites from moray eels produce puncture wounds, cuts, pain, and bleeding. California morays do not inflict venomous bites.

FIRST AID: Clean and disinfect the wound. Serious wounds may require suturing. If that is the case, get medical attention.

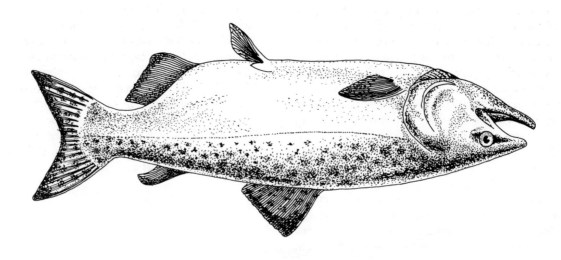

SALMON *Oncorhynchus* spp.

DESCRIPTION: There are 5 species of salmon found along our coast. All salmon have a small fleshy fin on the back between the dorsal fin and tail fin. To spawn, a salmon leaves the ocean and swims upstream, usually in the stream in which it was born. During the spawning season salmon go through physical changes. In some species, theses changes include the development of a hooked jaw and the enlargement of front teeth.

HAZARD: Salmon teeth are dangerous especially to fishermen attempting to remove hooks. These fish bite the unwary.

PREVENTION: Handle salmon with care avoiding the mouth and teeth.

SYMPTOMS: A bite by a salmon may produce puncture wounds, cuts, pain, and bleeding.

FIRST AID: Clean the wound and disinfect it. Get medical attention if cuts are severe or if infection develops.

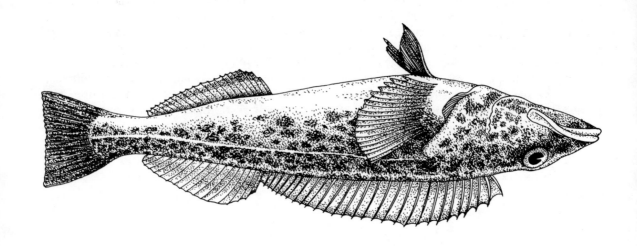

LINGCOD *Ophiodon elongatus*

DESCRIPTION: Lingcod are grayish-brown to greenish-blue fish with spotting along the back and sides. They have large mouths and long, sharp caninelike teeth. These fish can grow to 60 inches (1.5 m) in length and are found around rocky reefs inshore to 1400 feet (427 m). Although flesh of the lingcod often has a greenish tint, there is nothing wrong with the meat, and the color usually disappears when cooked.

HAZARD: Lingcod have very sharp and dangerous teeth. Fishermen have been bitten by them. Lingcod also have sharp gill rakers (small projections on the gills). These can cut fingers if handled.

PREVENTION: Handle lingcod with extreme care. Avoid placing fingers in the mouth or under the gill covers.

SYMPTOMS: Lingcod bites can cause puncture wounds, cuts, bleeding and pain. The gill rakers can cause cuts and bleeding.

FIRST AID: Clean and disinfect the wounds. If suturing is needed or if infection develops, get medical attention.

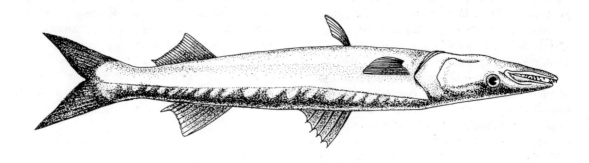

BARRACUDA *Sphyraena argentea*

DESCRIPTION: The barracuda has been called "the garden hose with teeth." Barracudas are long, thin fish that are dark brown along the back and silver along the underside. They are commonly found from the surface to about 60 feet (18 m) deep in warm waters. Barracudas grow to about 4 feet (1.2 m) in length.

HAZARD: Barracudas have mouths full of needle-sharp teeth. They have been known to bite fishermen trying to remove a hook. In some areas of the world barracudas are believed to attack divers. (Like all fish they are attracted to shiny objects.) Attacks on divers along our coast are unknown. Barracudas are very slimy fish. Contact with the slime does cause an allergic reaction in some people.

PREVENTION: Handle a barracuda with extreme care, especially when removing hooks from the mouth. Divers should not harass, provoke, or spear large barracudas. Cover any shiny objects when in the water.

SYMPTOMS: Barracuda bites can cause puncture wounds, cuts, bleeding, and pain. Contact with the slime may produce itching.

FIRST AID: Clean and disinfect bites. If suturing is needed, get medical attention. If an itch develops after handling a barracuda, wash the area with soap and water.

SHEEPHEAD *Semicossyphus pulcher*

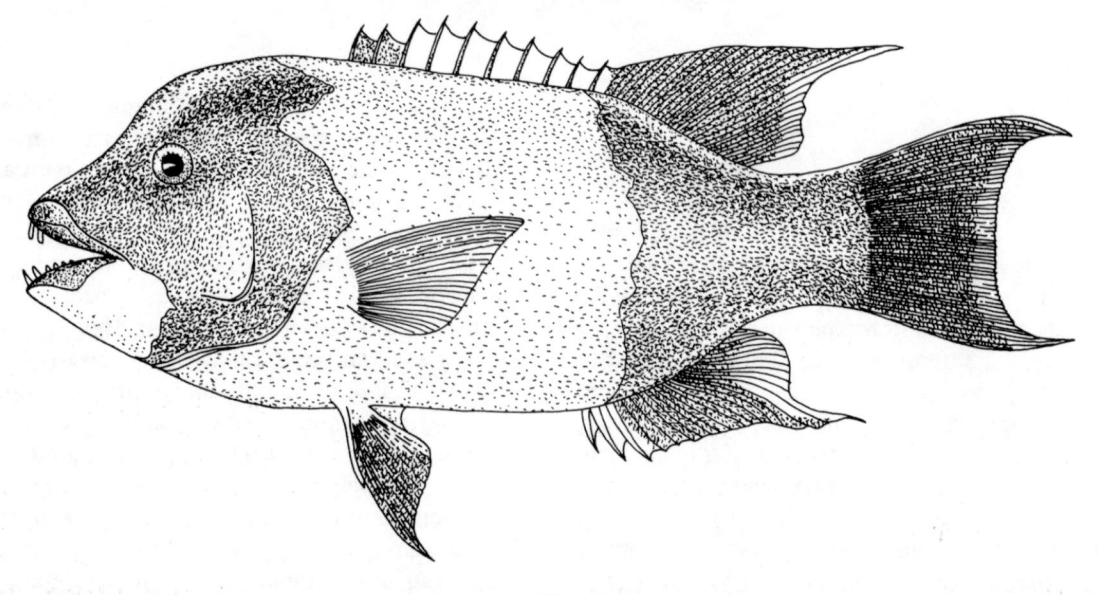

DESCRIPTION: Sheephead change color and sex as they get older. Juveniles are solid orange-red and have several dark roundish spots on the fins. Females are dull red to rose. Males have a black head and tail and a reddish midsection. Adult sheephead start as females, then become males later in life. Sheephead, especially the males, have sharp, stout teeth in the front of the mouth and strong, crushing ones toward the back of the mouth. Sheephead can grow to 3 feet (1 m) in length. They occur in kelp beds from shallow water to 180 feet (55 m).

HAZARD: The large teeth of the sheephead can cause serious bite wounds.

PREVENTION: Handle a sheephead very carefully; keep your fingers out of its mouth.

SYMPTOMS: A bite from a sheephead may produce puncture wounds, cuts, bleeding, and pain.

FIRST AID: Clean the wound and disinfect it. If suturing is needed or if the wound becomes infected, get medical attention.

WOLF-EEL *Anarrhichthys ocellatus*

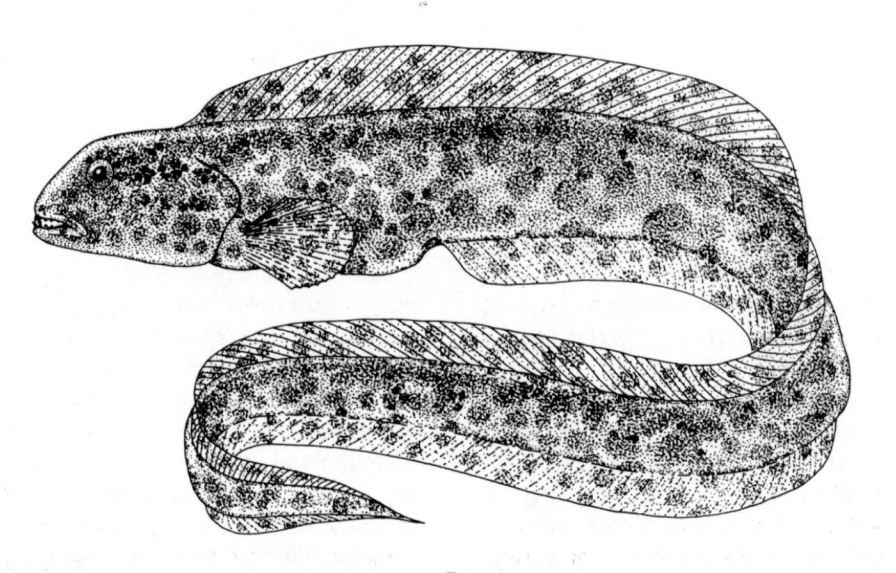

DESCRIPTION: Like the moray eel, the wolf-eel has an eel-like body; however, unlike the moray, this fish does have pectoral fins. The head of the wolf-eel is round and the mouth is full of sharp, white teeth and molars. The body color is grayish with circular spots covering the entire body. The wolf-eel grows to about 7 feet (2 m) in length. It is usually found from the shore to about 400 feet (120 m) in rocky crevices and caves.

HAZARD: The wolf-eel looks much more dangerous than it is. If provoked, it can inflict a serious bite, causing large tear-wounds that require medical attention.

PREVENTION: Do not provoke or spear a wolf-eel. If hooked, cut the line or use extreme care.

SYMPTOMS: A bite by a wolf-eel may produce wounds, cuts, tears, pain, and bleeding.

FIRST AID: Clean the wound and disinfect it. If suturing is needed, get medical attention.

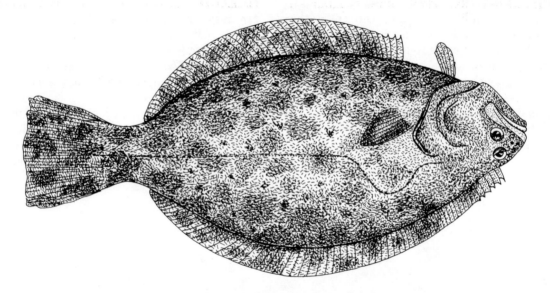

CALIFORNIA HALIBUT *Paralichthys californicus*

DESCRIPTION: The California halibut is a flatfish; that is, it is greatly flattened and lives most of its life lying on its side on the ocean floor. These fish can be identified by the large mouth filled with sharp teeth and by the high arch of the lateral line over the pectoral fin (see the picture). Halibut grow to 5 feet (1.5 m). Halibut are common on sandy or muddy bottoms from the surf zone to about 300 feet (100 m).

HAZARD: The California halibut has a mouth full of very sharp teeth. These fish will bite. This usually occurs when a fisherman is trying to unhook this fish.

PREVENTION: Handle a halibut with care, especially when unhooking a freshly caught one.

SYMPTOMS: Halibut bites can produce punctures, cuts, bleeding, and pain.

FIRST AID: Clean and disinfect the wound. If suturing is needed, get medical attention.

Fishes That Shock

PACIFIC ELECTRIC RAY *Torpedo californica*

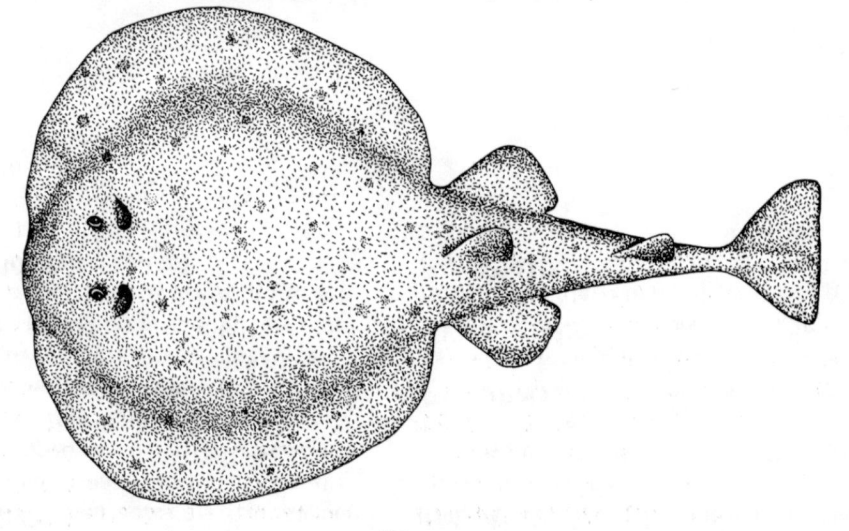

DESCRIPTION: The Pacific electric ray has a flattened body or disk, like other rays; however, its body is very round and flabby. There are no spines on the disk. The Pacific electric ray may reach a maximum length of 4.5 feet (1.4 m). This ray is gray along the backside and white on the underside. It is usually found resting or swimming over sandy or muddy areas in shallow waters to 650 feet (about 200 m).

HAZARD: As the common name implies, the Pacific electric ray can produce an electrical shock of up to 80 volts.

PREVENTION: Do not touch, handle or provoke a Pacific electric ray. The shock is produced at the rim of the disk.

SYMPTOMS: As with any electrical shock breathing may be interrupted and the person may become unconscious or paralyzed.

FIRST AID: If breathing should stop, immediately give mouth-to-mouth resuscitation or CPR until breathing resumes and get medical attention immediately.

III
SEA SNAKES

GREEN SEA SNAKE *Pelamis platurus*

DESCRIPTION: This is the only sea snake found off our coast. In general they are warm temperate and tropical water reptiles of the Pacific and Indian oceans. The body of the sea snake is compressed, with a flat, paddle-shaped tail for swimming. They are usually found in sheltered coastal waters, especially near the mouths of rivers. They live in fairly shallow waters because they eat bottom-dwelling animals and must come to the surface periodically to breathe. A sea snake's average length is about 4 feet (1.2 m).

HAZARD: Sea snakes possess a very potent venom and will bite to protect themselves. They have two or more fangs. Most people are bitten when they accidentally step on a sea snake or while trying to remove a snake from a fishing net. Provoked sea snakes have been known to bite divers. The aggressiveness of a sea snake depends on the species (some are more aggressive than others), the time of year, and the manner in which they are approached.

PREVENTION: Avoid swimming or diving near river mouths in sea snake areas. Do not handle or provoke a sea snake.

SYMPTOMS: There is little pain associated with the wound from a sea snake bite. Symptoms are usually more generalized and appear within a few minutes to a few hours after the bite. Most people who think they have been bitten by a snake panic and often go into shock. Sea snake bite symptoms include a stiffness and aching of the muscles, speaking and swallowing difficulties, progressive muscle paralysis, coldness and sweating, nausea, and vomiting. About 3 per cent of the victims die, usually of breathing paralysis. Complete recovery may take weeks to months.

FIRST AID: Determine if the victim has been bitten. Look for several pinhead-size puncture wounds. Keep the victim quiet and reclining, and cover to prevent heat loss. Immobilize the bitten area and keep lower than the victim's heart. Apply a constricting band (not a tourniquet) about 2-4 inches above bite (between bite and heart). This is to slow venom flow, not to stop blood flow. Clean wound and apply a bandage. Get the victim to medical attention immediately. A sea snake bite is a medical emergency.

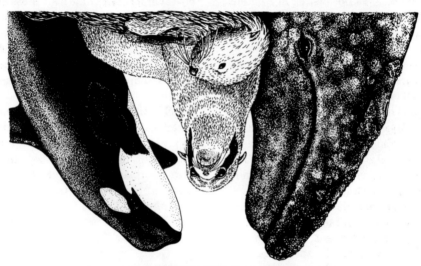

IV

MARINE MAMMALS

DESCRIPTION: Marine mammals along this coast include whales, seals, sea lions, and sea otters, with polar bears and walrus occurring off Alaska.

HAZARD: Many large marine mammals are predators. Due to their sizes and their hunting abilities, they can be hazardous to humans. This is especially true of seals and sea lions. During their breeding season, some seals and sea lions crowd beaches. The males become territorial and will defend their areas against all intruders, including humans. Marine mammals with young can also be dangerous if they feel threatened. Gray whales were called devilfish by hunters because of their ability to defend themselves with their powerful tail flukes.

PREVENTION: Do not provoke, harass or play with any marine mammal, especially mothers with their young. Divers should be careful when diving near seal or sea lion rookeries.

SYMPTOMS: Many marine mammals can inflict serious bite wounds, which are immediately evident.

FIRST AID: Wash the bite wound. Stop any bleeding with direct pressure over the wound. Get medical attention for suturing the wound and for antibiotics.

Appendices

FIRST AID KIT CONTENTS

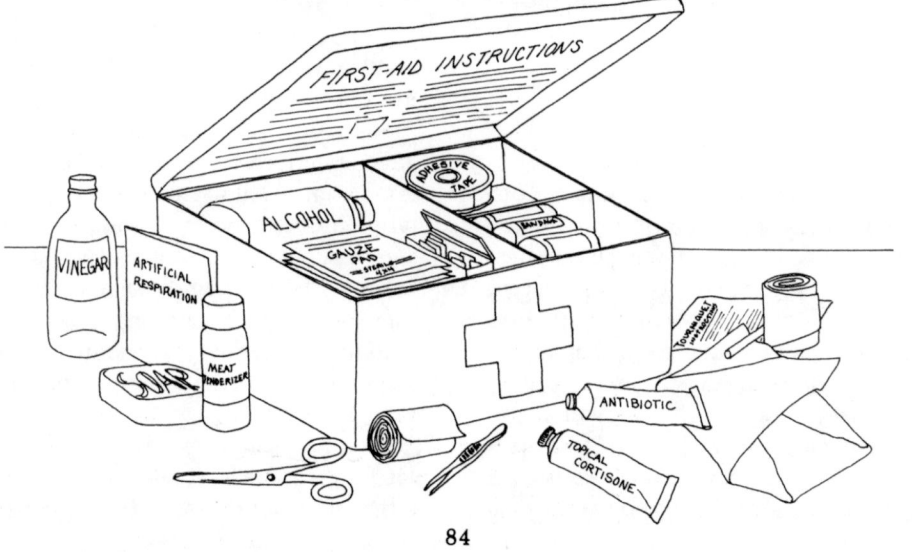

Many people who would automatically take a first aid kit on a hike into the mountains or the desert don't think about the hazards of the sea shore. You should always carry a first aid kit with you to the beach.

A first aid kit doesn't do any good unless you know how to use it. Be thoroughly familiar with the contents of your kit and keep the kit well supplied. You should also have some training in first aid procedures. Your local chapter of the American Red Cross can provide you with information on first aid classes. Following is a listing of items your first aid kit should contain:

instructions on first aid procedures
instructions on giving CPR
   and artificial respiration
soap
isopropyl alcohol
vinegar
meat tenderizer with papain
topical antibiotic
topical cortisone
gauze pads (3 or 4 inch squares)
gauze roll (1 to 3 inches wide)
triangular bandage
bandages (gauze with tape)
tape (adhesive)
scissors
tweezers
tourniquet with instructions

WHERE TO GET MEDICAL ATTENTION

If you have a victim that needs immediate medical attention, do not leave the victim unattended. While one person stays with the victim, another can get a doctor or ambulance.

If you are alone with the victim, do not leave him or her unless he or she is breathing normally. Do not leave a victim who is not breathing. If the victim is not breathing, get the person breathing before going for help. You should know how to administer cardiopulmonary resuscitation (CPR).

The telephone is your best tool for getting medical help. If you have an emergency, you can dial:

911 — (if available in your area) for police, fire and rescue units, or an ambulance;

0 — for an operator who can connect you with the necessary emergency services you need;

_____ — for the local poison control center. You should have this number in your first aid kit
(fill in and by your phone at home, also. You can get the number for the poison control cen-
phone #) ter in your area by calling Directory Assistance (411) or from the front of your phone
book. A poison control center can give you emergency information about poisonings,
poisonous substances, and venomous injuries.

_____ — for the nearest trauma center or hospital emergency treatment center. If you are tak-
(fill in ing a victim to the hospital, you may want to inform them of the emergency.
phone #)

_____ — for your family physician.
(fill in
phone #)

MARINE LIFE PROTECTED BY LAW

Many marine animals are protected by laws and if you disregard these laws, your pocketbook can be injured. Some laws limit the number of animals you can catch and keep; others regulate the size of a "legal" animal. Although some protected species are covered below, you should consult the most recent Fish and Game regulations pamphlet for current regulations in your area.

DESCRIPTION: The Garibaldi is the only brilliant orange fish along this coast. It frequents kelp beds and shallow-water reefs, but can be found at a maximum depth of 95 feet (30 m). Because these fish are territorial, they will stand and defend their ground. This makes them easy to approach underwater. Juvenile Garibaldi have iridescent blue blotching. Garibaldi can grow to a maximum length of 14 inches (35 cm).

HAZARD: The Garibaldi is fully protected by California state law. It is illegal to capture or kill these fish.

GARIBALDI *Hypsypops rubicunda*

GIANT SEA BASS, GULF and BROOMTAIL GROUPERS
Stereolepis gigas and *Mycteroperca* spp.

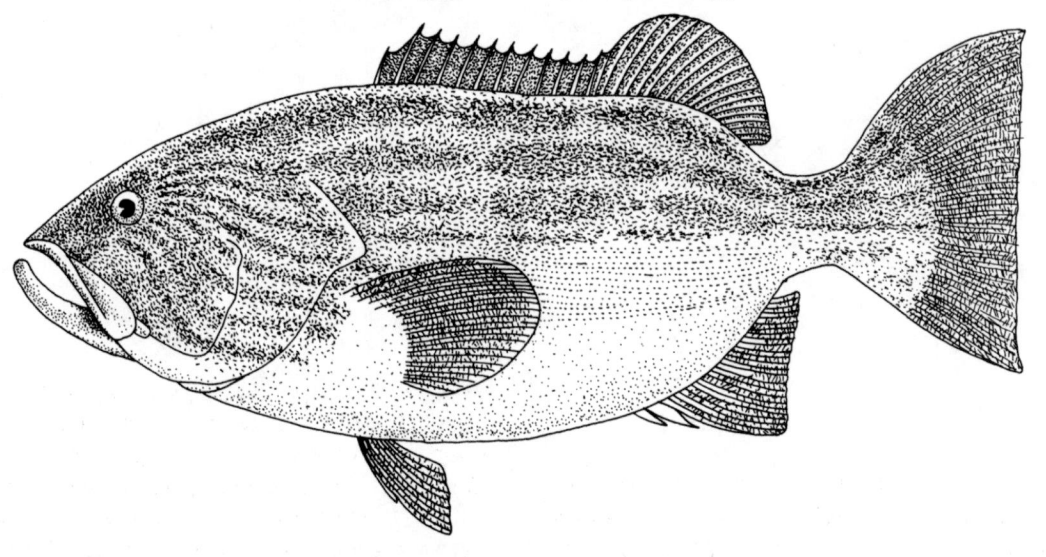

DESCRIPTION: These groupers are mostly plain brown to gray. They have the large broad mouth typical of most groupers. These fish can grow to 4-6 feet (1-2 m) in length. Although these fish are more common in warmer waters, a small population occurs off the California coast.

HAZARD: The giant sea bass, gulf and broomtail groupers are fully protected by law. It is illegal to capture or kill these fish.

Recommended Reading

Allen, Richard K. *Common Intertidal Invertebrates of Southern California.* rev. ed. Palo Alto, CA: Peek Publications, 1976.

Baxter, John L. *Inshore Fishes of California.* 5th rev. ed. Sacramento: Dept. Fish and Game, 1981.

Budker, Paul. *Life of Sharks.* New York: Columbia University Press, 1971.

Carlisle, John G., Jr. *Red Tide in California.* Marine Resources Leaflet #2. Sacramento: Dept. Fish and Game, 1968.

Castro, Joe I. *The Sharks of North American Waters.* College Station, TX: Texas A&M University Press, 1983.

Eschmeyer, William N., Earl S. Herald, and Howard Hammann. *A Field Guide to Pacific Coast Fishes of North America.* Boston: Houghton Mifflin Company, 1983.

Fitch, John E. *Offshore Fishes of California.* 5th rev. ed. Sacramento: Dept. Fish and Game, 1974.

_____ and Robert J. Lavenberg. *Marine Food & Game Fishes of California.* Berkeley: UC Press, 1975.

_____. *Tidepool & Nearshore Fishes of California.* Berkeley: UC Press, 1974.

Gotshall, Daniel W. *Pacific Coast Inshore Fishes.* Los Osos, CA: Sea Challengers and Ventura, CA: Western Marine Enterprises, 1981.

_____ and Laurence L. Laurent. *Pacific Coast Subtidal Marine Invertebrates: A Fishwatcher's Guide.* Los Osos, CA: Sea Challengers, 1979.

Halstead, Bruce W., M.D. *Poisonous & Venomous Marine Animals of the World.* rev. ed. Princeton: The Darwin Press, Inc., 1978.

_____. *Dangerous Marine Animals That Bite, Sting, Shock, Are Non-Edible.* 2nd ed. Maryland: Cornell Maritime Press, 1980.

Hinton, Sam. *Seashore Life of Southern California.* Berkeley: UC Press, 1969.

Iversen, Edwin S. and Renate H. Skinner. *How to Cope with Dangerous Sea Life.* Miami: Windward Publishing Co., 1977.

McLean, James H. *Marine Shells of Southern California.* rev. ed. Los Angeles: Nat. Hist. Museum Science Series # 24, 1978.

Miller, Daniel J. and Robert N. Lea. *Guide to the Coastal Marine Fishes of California.* Fish and Game Bulletin # 157. Sacramento: Dept. Fish and Game, 1972.

Morris, Robert H., Donald P. Abbott, and Eugene C. Haderlie. *Intertidal Invertebrates of California.* Stanford: Stanford U Press, 1980.

Moser, Mike, Milton Love, and Judy Sakanari. *Common Parasites of California Marine Fish.* Sacramento: Dept. of Fish and Game, 1983.

North, Wheeler J. *Underwater California.* Berkeley: UC Press, 1976.

Ricketts, Edward F. and Jack Calvin. *Between Pacific Tides.* 4th ed. rev. by Joel W. Hedgpeth. Stanford: Stanford U Press, 1968.

Russell, Findlay E. *Marine Toxins and Venomous and Poisonous Marine Animals.* New York: T.F.H. Publications, Inc., Ltd., 1971.

Sumich, James L. *An Introduction to the Biology of Marine Life.* Dubuque, IA: Wm. C. Brown Company Publishers, 1976.

Turner, Charles H. and Jeremy C. Sexsmith. *Marine Baits of California.* 1st rev. ed. Sacramento: Dept. Fish and Game, 1967.

Index